Coffee for Meg

Coffee for Meg

Poems by

Jonathan Cohen

© 2025 Jonathan Cohen. All rights reserved.
This material may not be reproduced in any form, published,
reprinted, recorded, performed, broadcast,
rewritten or redistributed without
the explicit permission of Jonathan Cohen.
All such actions are strictly prohibited by law.

Cover design by Shay Culligan
Cover image by Yahedoba
Author photo by Chris Bartlett/Bartlett Studios

ISBN: 979-8-90146-704-6

Kelsay Books
502 South 1040 East, A-119
American Fork, Utah 84003
Kelsaybooks.com

*Dedicated to Clara
with love and affection*

Acknowledgments

For support and encouragement, thank you: Jon Davis, Mark Goldman, Sam Magavern, Adele Evershed, Michael Collins, and Sam Adams.

Many thanks to these publications and their editors:

Cider Press Review: "Between the Tides"

Cloudbank Journal: "Psychedelia's Enduring Power to Disrupt Public Order"

Great Lakes Review: "Going to Seed"

History Highlights: "The Wave Leaves Buffalo Harbor, August 1, 1836"

Image Journal: "Inversion"

Little Patuxent Review: "After the Storm, Neighbors Examine the Damage"

Minyan Magazine: "Do Not Recede"

Ralph Angel Poetry Prize 2024 Runner Up: "Loon Sonnet"

SALT: "Coffee for Meg at the Utica Lounge"

Contents

Coffee for Meg at the Utica Lounge	13
Napping at a Family Gathering by Lake Erie	16
At the Dying Bed in the Summer House	18
Loon Sonnet	21
Psychedelia's Enduring Power to Disrupt Public Order	22
The Other Boy	24
Interrupted Wedding on a Warm Summer Night in a Small River Town Upstate	26
U.S. 89	27
The *Wave* Leaves Buffalo Harbor, August 1, 1836	29
Sam "The Mad Bomber" Melville Ponders the Future While Walking Home from His Job at the Bowling Alley on a Winter Night in Buffalo, NY, 1955	32
Going to Seed	34
Between the Tides	36
Requiem for a Chestnut Tree	37
After a Storm, Neighbors Examine the Damage	40
Marco Prepares His Car for Sale	41
Chet Baker on the Hotel Room Radio	42
Inversion	44
Famous Poet Withdraws His Signature from a Letter of Protest	45
Dreaming of Poland	47
Do Not Recede	50

*The purling river passes, and not its sound,
which is ours, not the river's.*

—Fernando Pessoa

Coffee for Meg at the Utica Lounge

In Memoriam

Runt in a ruddy line of consequential men,
unprepossessing, diabetic, slight.
He played the horses at a pharmacy
on Mohawk until they opened the OTB,
bought a weekly number at the bodega
on Virginia, knew where men made deals,
had an *easy drink or a quick bite,*
got things done with minimal fuss. Lived
in veteran's housing across the street—
short rise postwar brick and white trim building,
discordant among the old Victorians. His
brothers kept a desk for him at the family plant.

He took his meals here, more sitting room
than diner, soft lights, knock-off Persian
carpet. Not like the hash-slinging joint
down the street, noisy as a trading pit,
nor grief-stricken like Your Host,
the lamented local chain lit like a Hopper
painting. Here he could check the *Courier*
and the *News,* sometimes consult the *Journal,*
make notes in the racing form, *have a word.*

Meg, Meggy, Emmanuel—"God is with us,"
from the Hebrew—turned up quietly, gently
at family gatherings. Constant grey
pin-striped suit, white-on-white shirt—
smart, not showy, gold flex-bracelet watch,
black ankle boots, thin hair—colorless
filaments swept back on a smooth rising pate.

He always found the comfortable chair.
Had silver dollars for the kids, advice
if he liked you. *Don't take that to school,
hide it good.* Later, a demonstration
of how to clean pocket money: *fold the bills
lengthwise in your hand, like making a tent, you see?
Smooth away the wrinkles. Fold them all together
in half with the smallest denomination as the wrapper,
like this. Don't show too much; that's your roll.*
Much later, hearing us talk about a wild story
in the paper—*That knife fight down on Maryland?
The big guy who got killed, he was a friend
of your grandfather. It was a long time ago.
The cutter, they said he was a midget. Do me a favor,
boys, stay out of the Lower West Side.*

Land of slick suits and hard men, of chance,
risk, and stories to tell. We headed there
in an old Buick as soon as we could, to the Blue
Orchid and the No Name, sometimes
just a detour on the way to somewhere else,
to look for Meg, to find an irradiating gleam,
faint but certain, illumining his secret world.

Napping at a Family Gathering by Lake Erie

The setting is key—a picnic
on the porch of a beach house
overlooking the lake, a gaggle
chattering about nothing
special, which leads to the use

of a few magic words that open
a portal. My cousin Judi
remembers the many acorns
the old oak once showered on the lawn
and wonders why the yield is so small.

Acorns on the lawn carries us back
to when we played here as children.
Savor of lake water dampness conjures itself,
perfumes the wood chest still here,
though no longer present, filled with jai alai

and badminton sets, my grandfather holding
court at an Amish-style card table in a T-Shirt
and suspenders, sipping whiskey, bantering
with brothers and friends, sharing slices
of cheesecake, my grandmother and aunts

clearing dishes, gossiping, the coffee
brewing. *Cheesecake and voices.* I've slipped
into the house to nap on the cracked leather couch,
drifting on the warm air. Richard and Michael's
baritones rise above the din; I hear their father,
my great uncles. Everything sounds important.

I am seven years old. My aunt Molly leads me to bed
in the room she shared with my mother in the back
of the house, wallpapered with a boy and girl
standing among tulips, lace curtains gesturing.

In the cat's paw breeze voices carry
to the room. Molly whispers, "You're not
missing anything, believe me." She tucks me
into crisp white sheets. My mother comes
to say goodnight. She is beautiful. She loves me.

At the Dying Bed in the Summer House

After Delmore Schwartz

At the dying bed in the summer house,
the southwest wind blows heavily
from the lake, footsteps
come and go on the back porch,
the dog scratches at the door.
Neighbors arrive in bicycle gear
and gardening clothes, sit quietly,
leave quietly. An old friend appears
from nowhere, prays at bedside,
disappears.

> *Truck wheels cue a jangle of displaced stones,*
> *clomping boots, mowers thudding to the ground.*

On the beach a tractor turns,
gathering algae in shifting piles, raking
and raking the sand, its rider giving no
attention to the sailboat foundering at anchor
just feet from shore, the bent mast wedged
beneath a rock, the rigging and buckles
exposed to waves and wind.

The relatives talk in low tones about
the local wildlife. The fox that prowls
the beach at night. The protected toads
threatened by the loss of American beachgrass.
The air grows chill, the dog chuffs shallow
draughts of scent as someone shuts the door.

Observing the flailing sheets, I mark a page,
rise from the chair, check my phone
and let the dog out again.

The sun glints through trees—the battered
sugar maple that anchors the dune, the cottonwoods that root in
sand like weeds—then loses itself behind tottering clouds.

A presence struggles to form
in the windswept room. There is moaning,
outstretched legs, knees bent in a birthing posture,
the small of the back thrust forward,
haunches exposed, daring the universe
to urge something into the world once more—a final delivery.
The women scurry to undress her, turn her, swab her,
stroke her clenching face, look past her empty stare.

A whirring motor and the smell of gasoline
from the world outside. Inside, memory summons
older, softer sounds.

A long-ago milkman's footfall
on the formerly manicured walk,
the groan of rusty well-water pumps,
the lingering murmur of long departed
dinner guests, the clinking of plates
being cleared, a neighbor's *hallo* laced
with a bit of sarcasm hanging in the air

for decades, joyful children careering
into the lake. Even the happy boy two houses
down, who grew into a troubled life, failed
the service, died in a car accident, will always be
chasing his dog on the beach,
pulling the string of his toy boat
of nailed-together scrap wood
through splashing waves,
laughing into the sky.

How can we forgive the past when even
its thinnest tendrils grip the present?
When the sounds in the yard have finally died,
do they follow us to our long home?
Or just echo faintly through the cosmos—
unreceived signals forever pinging Jupiter
and Mars, the severed cord rippling free
at the dimming center of creation.

Loon Sonnet

We drove through spectral Adirondack towns
to an RV camp on Loon Lake, off-season, empty,
cold and damp, Raisinets and Twizzlers
at the concession, slept in a moldy canvas tent.
Missed the loons. Summer, we tried again, biking
to Crystal Beach, using only backroads, no main vias,
took field paths, short cuts through private yards,
startled tennis players. No loons. But down one
long driveway, the playwright's house—stone
pigs on the wall, behind it, the romantic brick house
decaying under vines, and nearby, the red-tiled roof
of the poet's home, an idling mini-bike capsized in the grass.
That fall, we planned our garden—zinnias,
bergamot, the blue flag iris that edged Loon Lake.

Psychedelia's Enduring Power to Disrupt Public Order

In the parking lot at Lowe's, after I've loaded
seven bags of mulch for Clara's garden,
the one-hit wonder *I Had Too Much to Dream (Last Night)*
drifts from my car radio like a whisper, then blasts out
urgently, turned up loud for everyone to hear,
to be reminded that a strange, bombastic song
can become a Top 40 hit, pierce the veil of, you know,
bourgeois respectability.

Consider what it was like at 8:30 drive time, third Tuesday,
November 1966, when Kathy the secretary and Mark
the junior insurance man, and who knows who,
headed to work in their Fairlanes and Valiants,
listening to the commuter shows—Sandy Beach on WKBW
or Mark Melody on WNIA—heard for the first time
the warped feedback wobble of the Electric Prunes.
What did they think as they strained to grasp the lyrics
and the story—if that's what it was—a soured romance
or wait, an *acid trip* gone wrong? They had read about those.
How did the rest of their day go? Did they get through ok
or quit their jobs, minds blown there and then? How long did it
take *turn on, tune in, drop out,* and *sha la la la la la live for today?*

Where are Kathy and Mark now?
On the street in the Tenderloin? A hospice
in White Plains? Living their best lives in the *Villages?* What
comes to mind when they hear on a radio, as I do today,
sitting in the Lowe's parking lot with seven bags of mulch,
that oscillating vibrato issue from cheap plastic speakers
embedded in the door, panels shaking
as the volume builds, and you can't help but turn it up,
threatening to tear apart the delicate grey paper cones within.
Where are any of us, for that matter, stuck between
the world of our dreams and the one of matter-in-motion?

The Other Boy

I wish I'd been a boy who knew
the names of dinosaurs and stars,
of Roman generals. A boy who
refracted light through beakers,
read the unabridged *Count of Monte Cristo,*
easily mastered French declensions,
knew the different theories
of Darwin, Agassiz, Lamarck.
But I was a boy entranced
by radio stations that reverbed
their DJs' voices, ran "Paul is Dead"
specials at Halloween. I was a boy
who followed the big kids into trouble,
transfixed by jeans-clad, patchouli-
scented girls who rolled
in the playing fields after dinner,
grogging up Orange Mist, waving
menthols like wands. A boy
who wanted all the girls to adore him.
What if I had been the other boy?
Would I have aced the SATs and gone to Harvard,
partnered at a private equity firm,
served a government appointment,
married a thin blond dressed in Lilly Pul
with exquisite taste in furnishings,

who could tie a fly and drop it tight
behind a boulder? Would I have fathered
two boys, two girls, all varsity lacrosse?
Would my summer home be on MV
or in the OBX? Or, waking at 4:30
on April mornings before driving
my Porsche Macan to work, listening
to *The Meditations,* would I wonder
about this other me, the crazy things
I did with my hoodlum friends,
and revel in the promise
of those patchouli-scented girls
lingering still in autumn air,
before the gentle snow that never fully falls.

Interrupted Wedding on a Warm Summer Night in a Small River Town Upstate

Alarm ringing from the neighboring hotel,
we wend from the brick factory turned banquet hall
guided by fireflies. No panic. Beside us, the silent,
broad lawn; mowed grass, balmy; the calm river
sliding through its bend like a magic serpent conferring
power and grace, a dragon of good fortune. Smiling
servers offer glasses, pour wine, the chatter
and laughter join immortal crosstalk. All the great parties
that ever were must have been like this, slow and easy,
gliding steps, poised footfalls along a gardened walk.
An unhurried call to return ripples among the guests,
no bells. Wives and husbands, romantic couples
snake under a bower, through double doors. What movie
is this, which ancient city? Playfully, they offer Hitchcock,
Fellini, Nice or Rome, a courtyard in Ferrara. Dinner is served
in the glowing hall, everyone smiling. Lights low, the band plays
a samba. Soon the dancing will start. The night
expands with the universe, gestures toward forever,
the soft flowing river, the wholehearted lights of the town.

U.S. 89

This is the road you have always driven.
The cloverleaf, the granite
cut between two interstates,
sun-glittered snow, protective mist
of snow squalls. When you drive through,
bright days leaving school early
for the winter hills are still on. You can
feel them. Rolling Stones in the tape deck,
wholesome girls in jeans and sweaters,
bandanas tied below their knees—*such a cool flourish.*
You tumble after them in a drifted gully,
steal kisses behind the lift house. There
was the summertime when you and
Gideon hitched across New England,
came this same way to a farm
in Woodstock. You swam w/ lovely
girls in a pond, spent an afternoon
in a barn telling stories—one had surfer
girl looks, the other a sultry voice.
You still drift on her cello-deep tone.
Lonely men drive the granite cut, too.
They offer rides to safe-seeming
hikers. James was in his 50s, work boots,
grey pants, plaid shirt, Eisenhower jacket,
mechanic's cap. Stopped his truck on a hot
afternoon, headed for New Hampshire. He talked
about his wife's cancer, and then of his Army days

in Australia. "A local guy cleaned our barracks,"
he said. "Blew the whole company."
James is still in the cut 60 years on,
looking for someone, driving through again
and again, never connecting.
The beach is rimed with crystals
you break with your boot heel,
a satisfying "pop" at the edge of the
Sound, which leads to a bight that
flows to the sea and to Portugal
and back around. There is a big
football game on TV. A player
quotes Heraclitus to his teammates:
"It's not the same river," he exhorts.
"We are not the same men."
You look out over the empty water—
nothing but oyster boats.
Snow is falling in the mountains.
You gather your things, load the car,
head for U.S. 89.

The *Wave* Leaves Buffalo Harbor, August 1, 1836

No one knows who James Dickson was;
no one knows what became of him.
   —Bernard DeVoto, Across the Wide Missouri

Tailored coat wine-stained from the investors'
dinner on the Canadian side down river
where eloquence and huzzahs can re-course history,
epaulets weighing the humid afternoon,

he dismounts his host's carriage, brain lolling
the thorn of insult stuck by the British consul:
Filibuster? No, liberator,

and raising a bone-handled cane,
Excalibur from the stone, shouting to the troops
hunkered in a field by the docks, who chant
the Sun Dance, drink corn, throw dice,
General Dickson launches his oratory.

"From here LaSalle embarked
to take the north for France and cast us out.
Likewise, we sail for the hinterlands
that arrogant DeSoto claimed for Spain, ceded
to the Comanche, eaters of mice, beggars of offal;
we raise our Metis army at Red River and with mighty
blows break the slavery of Cortez."

The words in his saber-scarred
cheeks won't stop fluttering,
fatted quail that fly to heaven,
retrieve anointment, beat themselves
dead with their own frantic wings.

The crowded dock is slick with grease.
Stevedores hump cargo from packets and barques,
voices of New York, Quebec, the Ohio Valley.
Someone sings the Red River ballad.

They laugh at Montezuma II, call a fiddler
to play another reel, bid the girls
outside the tavern dance, crack wise
about the schooner, its rot visible on the bowsprit.
"They'll never make it to the Soo."

Ravenous at Kelly's Island, they roast
three cows; at Detroit, Apollo takes
revenge by agency of the local sheriff.
The General leaves six of the crew in jail,
sells the *Wave* for scrap. Overland
to the Minnesota wilderness, marching north
toward Santa Fe, the scouts slip off.

Lost in October's violent snow, bone-chill,
fathomless, Dickson can see the mesas,
hear the chirr of the fortune-bearing blackbird,
but there are no wings, or words now,
only the liberation of bankrupt sleep.

Sam "The Mad Bomber" Melville Ponders the Future While Walking Home from His Job at the Bowling Alley on a Winter Night in Buffalo, NY, 1955

The clinker in my eye
cools to a gleaming gem,
a new color, a new way of seeing
beyond the interdiction
of grey skies draped
in snow and soot
from the tire plant.
Chemical fungus coats
rusting swing sets, corrodes
doorbell and door handle,
rusts mailboxes
stuffed with bills and notices.
The ember still penetrates,
my eye burns, unbearable.
I wander like Ishmael
along the dark and glistering
streets embanked like canals
in a polar sea that stretches and undulates,
undulates and stretches, the city
beckoning as a distant star
with an important message
from the farthest galaxies:
there are stars beyond the stars.

With this new eye forged
in poverty, I see a future
of recompense, avengement
for all the people ground
down and extruded to pay
for wars, police, country clubs,
hockey rinks, prostitution,
bars to keep working men
drunk and in debt, to keep
fathers from turning to their sons,
and sons to their fathers.
Listen, a new sun is rising,
a new dawn, past the heavens,
and I will be there to greet it.

Going to Seed

You making haste, haste on decay
—Robinson Jeffers

My neighbor's pocket garden is going to seed.
The morning glory, its lone white bloom,
has taken over the back fence that separates
our yards, the pumpkin vines run wild behind it,
untrammeled apple trees mass and reach, their ganglia
of twigs and leaves filling the white space
once there to dream on.
When he built it, we watched him lay down
the custom timbers that terrace and box
the vegetables, and carefully plant
the young fruit trees tagged for display.
Everyone praised his labor, the care he afforded
to shape this miniature Babylon.
Smartly designed and orderly, yielding
righteous crops in a small space, virtuous, gleaming,
the garden served as model for the neighbors,
inspiring and reproachful all at once. The small talk
about this or that planting piled up a silo's worth
of good will—(a cordiality, it might be noted, prized
as much for its limits as its social lubrication).

After the harvest and through the winter, wisps
of envy and imagined slights—squash falling
on the wrong side of the fence, the failure to consult
about the sleek, modern beehive wedged
on the property line—unsubstantial as smoke
in November's cold, drifted away by January.
Come March, the colony of rabbits who had taken
residence brazenly surged forth to graze the clover
and sweet young grass of the adjoining lawns,
a sign not of the garden's emergent fruitfulness
but its abandonment. This is the most enchanting
part, the overgrowth, the rusting barrow filled with rainwater,
the hoe and other tools left where they were last used, like a scene
from the retreat of a fallen army.

Between the Tides

Walk the shore with me
in this gleam, waked
by the young March wind
tantalizing our necks,
the estuary's revealed grasses
green and vernal,
sun slanting in the west
warming our backs, pushing
off winter and the weight of years.

We call each other to this light
as we called each other when we
were young and playful as ducks,
water trembling a golden edge,
anticipating its run over dappled
flats before the dark surge.

This is what I want before looking
back to sum our journey:
to hold back the turning tide
until we cannot last,
until the flood washes over us
and we are submerged again, earth
and sky separated, the west
wind moaning over our surrender.

Requiem for a Chestnut Tree

Thirty years and I noticed its presence
only this fall, the leaves narrow like no
others, dropped to the street by October
rain, and how they had turned crimson-brown,
gold flames flaring up the center, like
fingers reaching for the sun before its final
surrender to the implacable black hole
of its own making. So much already gone.
The shaved stump left after the arborists
had done their work, pulled back memory's
shade on the house across the street where
the Mennonite family lived, four young girls
and their mother, the quiet father, the rattling
Country Squire station wagon where they huddled
after he robbed a bank on a Wednesday
afternoon. They ran for it up the hill
behind the grade school among mansions,
old farmhouses, looking down on the Sound
and home and us before the police came.
Old Joe Quinn and his spinster sisters
no longer next door, dinner dishes clattering
through our window on a summer night,
to get the details straight about that
sad family, the McMansion built on the foundation
of the Quinn's house now on its third owner
since they passed. They left everything to the Church

except the tea set Rita gave our girls
when they were young and played beneath
the cherry tree between the yards, nightly
mason jar of Manhattans in her knurled hands.
Show me a man without vice, she would joyfully declare,
*and I'll show you a man without virtue. That's
what Father James always says.* And she would
toast my health and plot how she and her siblings
might get to the city to see *Riverdance.*
Virtue/virtuté/valor. Most of the men
on the street were ornery, their higher qualities
unapparent. Henry, the butcher yelling
at kids on the sea wall; the airline pilot,
Vinny, summoning the police if you parked
too long at the curb; Robert the retired Bronx
cop; and Wendy, his blind wife,
yelling out the back door at the sparrows.
Those guys got through just fine.
Paid the mortgage, raised their kids, managed
pathologies without fuss. That's valor.
They were old stock, like the chestnut tree,
one thousand left throughout the county,
like the lobster traps abandoned at the bottom
of the Sound, given way to new things,

handsome Lauro bushes and Belgian bloc
driveways, Hardie siding replacing asbestos.
I don't begrudge the new people
or how they've buffed the houses to a
shine, though I'd like to discuss it all
with Old Joe—the constancy, the change.

After a Storm, Neighbors Examine the Damage

Thunder exploded the sky last night, photo-electric
flashes scattered like salt and silver nitrate across
the deep black, sheets of rain washing it all
into a bright dawn. When morning dog walkers
meet along the path, the animals project their owners'
curiosity, strain to examine the offscourings and scraps
along the shore, tentatively step toward the flooded
seagrass, retreat at the scent of a raccoon carcass,
dead fish in the shallows. The walkers gaze out
and point at unmoored boats tossed on the rocks
like nautical debris—O'Connor's beautiful *Thistle,*
restored pristine, shining blue hull, gunwales
richly stained, now gashed on its port bow; a busted
catamaran hung with kelp, knocking against the seawall
like a ghost. The bottom quarter of the propeller shaft
on Jimmy's Boston Whaler has snapped off, engine hood
swinging from a latch. Everyone stops to admire
a chalk-white tender lodged in the reeds, its delicate
wooden stars secure on the trim, oars nestled in their
locks like the crossed arms of a young athlete. *That's
a fine old boat,* someone says. *Look how it survived the storm!*

Marco Prepares His Car for Sale

Marco and Jeanine are fussing curbside
over his Shelby Cobra. He kept the car, a vintage '66—
growling 427 under the hood—on a lift in his garage.
A million-dollar car, mint condition, guardsman blue,

double white racing stripes decaling the hood
and rear, on each door, white discs, "66"
painted black. Years past, he would drive it
in the Memorial Day Parade, race it at Lime Rock,

detail it in the driveway of his blue frame home.
Now it's on a trailer, covered and trussed,
waiting. Marco, thin and hobbled is fighting
stomach cancer, the most painful kind they say—

wide snap-on suspenders hold up soiled jeans
on a wasting frame, shirttails swim
in the waistline's ebb, smoke-stained, ink-stained
fingers adjust trailer hitch, ratchet down ties.

Jeanine looks on, one hand loose on a leash,
the dog, Suzzy, unsure what to do.
A vacuum tube TV sits on the front porch,
not quite blocking the door, faint lines

burned into its gray screen. Marco limp-steps
up the curb away from the trailer, grunts,
"that should do it," takes the leash, wraps it
like phylacteries, walks Suzzy up the street.

Chet Baker on the Hotel Room Radio

You're listening to Chet Baker sing
"My Funny Valentine" on the radio
in a hotel room, biding time,
making work, before attending an event
you don't want to attend. Nonetheless,
here you are, perched in a room over
the hotel entrance, the cigarette can,
occasional gaggles of smokers
directly below your window.
The salesmen boast of deals nearly landed.
One says, "If I can get one more signed at 24,
I can get 25 next year for sure."
A manager, apparently—maybe an owner—
a woman of years, talks coarsely
of a company merger gone sideways.
"Seven million fucking dollars
on the fucking table, and they left it there.
Fucking cocks. Well, that's what they're for,
right?" So it goes, the world carries on
with its vain concerns, while you sit alone
with dust motes, extra towels,
Chet Baker of the limpid tone,
the hushed voice, son of Oklahoma

who could not read music, who,
looking for a fix, fell to his death
from a window in an Amsterdam flophouse,
who could produce the clearest, loneliest sound—
a hard luck case with nothing coarse about him.

Inversion

Waves of anger and fear
Circulate over the bright
And darkened lands of the earth
                —W. H. Auden

An inversion layer hangs over my neighborhood,
sounds carom off the ground, bounce the ether.
The tone is clear, the meaning jumbled.
Familiar voices—neighbors and friends,
dog walkers, yard workers, house painters, roofing
crews, fit loose and comfortably in my ears.
Mothers and nannies push prams; I hear them, too.
But I don't get what they are saying: *Stop the pesticide*
wings from the end of the street to the corner; *an illegal*
occultation pings garden buttresses, the curbs.
The response is extortionate, I seem to hear;
                    what they are doing is liminal.
An osprey drawn inland by the sound perches
on a dead maple, menacing the rabbits, eyeing
the nearby chickens. She is not confused by the inversion;
it suits just fine. Fences are down, restraints are off.
Her mask darkens, her beak sharpens, her eyes glint.
The voices drown the neighborhood in weird phrases.
From the silver to the scree. Gory to the starters.
                    Go back to lowland; we despise you still.
Jinking through the yards, a host of sparrows passes
from darkness to darkness.

Famous Poet Withdraws His Signature from a Letter of Protest

Dasha, there is a pit
in my stomach where usually
I feel only longing for you.
My poems, and all their prizes—
the Paris apartment,
the cottage in the forest
by the sea where the whales breach
and the eagles whistle—all of it,
I admit to you, my love,
drawn from stories of suffering
under Hitler and Stalin and the Tzars.
Such a rich tradition to mine,
to present in a new form,
universalizing pain and suffering,
human experience in all its
beauty and squalor, coping humor,
existential absurdity.
To set our delicate fragility
against the brutish calamity
of American armies
no different than rampaging
Cossacks. So necessary, important.

Between us, I am not ashamed
to say, it was a triumph of moral
imagination, the plaudits,
the awards, the dinners.
How could I not sign a simple letter
against the boycott of Jewish books?
Literary publishing houses are not
war machines. Am I right?
So with pride and humility, I signed
the letter. Yes, I signed it, only later
to realize who else had signed it,
and also who had not.
Dasha, do you understand?
I withdrew my golden name.

Dreaming of Poland

Jaschik cares for my father-in-law
in the house across the street,
bald and pale, thick-boned, squat,
came from Lodz at 43 knowing
little of America except the records
of Stevie Ray Vaughn. My mother
visits from a city famous
for its Polonia; she doesn't like Poles.
Her family came from Pruchnik,
known for jelly doughnuts, where kids
still beat an effigy of a Jew at Easter.

Jaschik knows that people make fun
of Poles. "They think we are dumb,"
he tells my wife, "but everyone makes
fun of everyone, so what does it matter.
I only care about Stevie Ray Vaughn
and the Blues." Jaschik makes borscht
and pierogi for my father-in-law, dying
slowly, hallucinating, a poster of an
Orthodox saint taped above his bed.
The beets, potatoes, shots of honey
vodka might be comforting, or make
him thick-tongued and slow. Lately,
Jaschik has been tying a kerchief
to the old man's head, pirate style.

The news of the world is dramatic.
Violent protests in the streets of every
major city. Flags and banners fly
in support of terrorist armies,
marchers chant, "death to Israel," sing
of a slaughter of Jews 1400 years ago.
Nations rise and fall on the TV,
hostages waste and die in hidden
prisons, tyrants flee and flail.

At a family dinner, my mother fidgets.
She interrogates Jaschik about his life
but she isn't interested, really. She speaks
nonsense to him *"Jak się masz,"* she says,
"Jak się masz, over an out!"
Mother is afraid of Jaschik but thinks
she can get over on him.
It's embarrassing. Jaschik doesn't
show anger. I try to distract my
mother, ask her about things back
home. She can't help herself, talks
about the Dyngus Day festival,
the Polish men who worked
alongside her father at the warehouse.

Jaschik prepares to take my father-in-law
home. As I help at the front door with coats,
the wheelchair, he asks if he can take our
family picture the next day. Jaschik is a big
photographer, he tells me, and would we
dress in traditional clothes with prayer
shawl and skullcap? I ignore him.

Pigeons and sparrows scrap over
a nearby birdfeeder—an ancient swirling
vortex—feathers scatter the driveway,
dusk settles cold as the day the Red Army
liberated Warsaw. My ill-behaved mother
potchkies in the kitchen. I have to confront
her but I just want to lie down, to dream
of Carpathian fields and forests, of ambling
bellflowered meadows, white and red.

Do Not Recede

After Isaac Bashevis Singer

Receiver of prayers, do not
recede into black holes, worm holes,
bending folds in space. Do not
reduce us to neurons,
algorithms, code. Remove
the dull film of blindered scientism,
rigid thought systems, superficial lists,
rushed conclusions, false certainties,
through which we see the world
more dimly than our ancestors.
Reverse in us a turned sense of wonder
at stars, oceans, mountains, all living things—
the snow owl that alighted, wings
aloft, on the roadside at dusk when we
were lost, the net pulled from the lilac
pond brimming, creatures wriggling through
our fingers, nipping our flesh. Restore in us
amazement at ourselves, each other, the beauty
of our form, the lightning bolt of connection
through a joke, a gesture, good talk. Return grandeur
to creation, a deserving crown to our heads.
Reject the daily news: despair, loneliness,
the overload, the-all-too-much.

Give us language to express our miraculous
circumstance, to recount the mystery
of our existence, unique in the cosmos
as far as we know, sacred so long as we insist,
here among the billions grown from the same
extraordinary seed, dependent on honor and hope,
chancing astonishment at what we have been given,
be there, not receding.

About the Author

Jonathan Cohen's recent poems appear in SALT, *Image, Little Patuxent Review,* and others. He is the author of *Work Songs* (Finishing Line Press) and a finalist for the Blue Lynx Prize.

www.ingramcontent.com/pod-product-compliance
Lightning Source LLC
Chambersburg PA
CBHW060034180426
43196CB00045B/2686